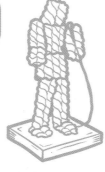

WHAT'S THE DEAL WITH
EVERYONE HIDING?

WHAT'S THE DEAL WITH EVERYONE HIDING?

A Seek-and-Find Book

ADAM BEECHEN
ILLUSTRATED BY MAXIM USIK

Running Press
PHILADELPHIA

Hachette Book Group supports the right to free expression and the value of copyright. The purpose of copyright is to encourage writers and artists to produce the creative works that enrich our culture.

The scanning, uploading, and distribution of this book without permission is a theft of the author's intellectual property. If you would like permission to use material from the book (other than for review purposes), please contact permissions@hbgusa.com. Thank you for your support of the author's rights.

Running Press
Hachette Book Group
1290 Avenue of the Americas, New York, NY 10104
www.runningpress.com
@Running_Press

First Edition: October 2024

Published by Running Press, an imprint of Hachette Book Group, Inc. The Running Press name and logo are trademarks of Hachette Book Group, Inc.

The Hachette Speakers Bureau provides a wide range of authors for speaking events. To find out more, go to www.hachettespeakersbureau.com or email HachetteSpeakers@hbgusa.com.

Running Press books may be purchased in bulk for business, educational, or promotional use. For more information, please contact your local bookseller or the Hachette Book Group Special Markets Department at Special.Markets@hbgusa.com.

The publisher is not responsible for websites (or their content) that are not owned by the publisher.

Print book cover and interior design by Frances J. Soo Ping Chow

ISBN: 978-0-7624-8779-0

Printed in China

1010

10 9 8 7 6 5 4 3 2 1

Contents

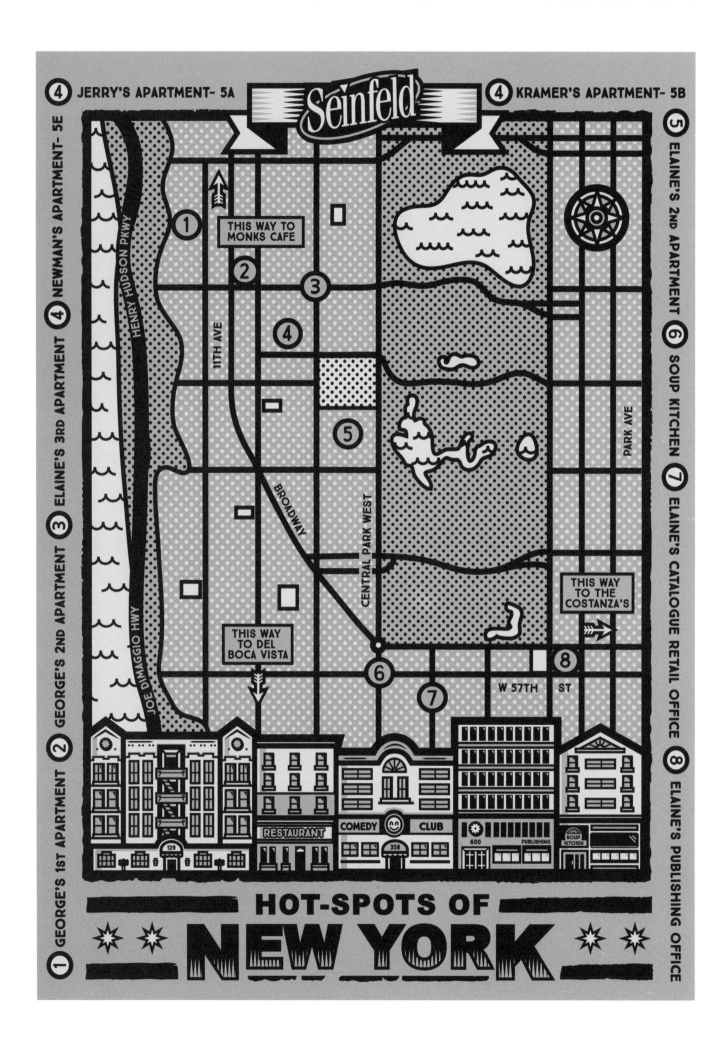

Introduction

Put on your finest puffy shirt, grab your astronaut pen, and practice your dance moves, because you've been invited to hang out with Jerry, Elaine, George, and Kramer! They may be a little hard to track down, however, because they're making the rounds of all their favorite haunts. You might catch up to them at the baseball game, at one of their apartments, visiting relatives, out for something to eat, or just running into recognizable faces they might or might not want to see.

But be prepared! You never know when you'll happen to meet a close talker or someone who you used to date whose name you can't remember. Then again, you might bump into someone who's actually sponge-worthy. You'll probably find all kinds of familiar things along your way.

You can take your time, however . . . Because when you do find our "heroes," chances are they'll just be complaining. Or scheming. Or worrying. Or doing nothing at all. You know, the same old "yada, yada, yada."

Jerry   Elaine   George   Kramer

JERRY'S APARTMENT

A burst pipe in Jerry's building has made life miserable for many residents, but Jerry's place isn't affected. Good Samaritan Kramer has invited everyone to Jerry's for relief. Even the Cuban cigar rollers have come! Now they're all eating Jerry's cereal, there's a long line for the bathroom, and Kramer's hiding from Jerry's wrath!

MONK'S CAFÉ

The "Big Salad Special" has packed the diner with hungry customers, and some of them are familiar faces. Is that an old boyfriend of Elaine's? How did Kramer already get a seat? And are the Bizarro versions of the gang trying to beat our heroes to their favorite booth?

J. PETERMAN CATALOG OFFICES

Jerry, Kramer, and George have stopped by Elaine's office, but it's J. Peterman's birthday and the place is packed with well-wishers wearing their favorite catalog items. Elaine has wisely run for cover as her boss holds court, regaling everyone in earshot with his tall tales.

13

JERRY'S PARENTS' DEL BOCA VISTA PHASE III COMMUNITY

Kramer has "retired" and moved into Jerry's parents' Florida development. He's running for president of the condo board, and there's a fundraiser in the clubhouse. But it's a rule violation to be barefoot in the clubhouse, and Kramer can't find his shoes! Maybe they're with Morty's missing tip calculator.

ELAINE'S APARTMENT

Elaine's indoor yard sale has attracted lots of interest, but Jerry's looking for the watch he left behind the last time he came over. Meanwhile, George is fighting a losing battle with the pricing gun, and Kramer's coffee table book is the hottest item of all. Everything must go!

GEORGE'S APARTMENT

With the possibility his building could be named a historical site, George wants to sublet his apartment for a fortune. Now there's realtors and prospective tenants everywhere; Jerry, Kramer, and Elaine are wandering around reminiscing; and George isn't so sure he wants to move after all . . .

ROYAL BAKERY/SCHNITZER'S

This morning, it seems like the entire city has come for their favorite sweets and baked goods. There's bickering over babka, battles over black-and-white cookies, and hollering over challah. Brunch is in serious jeopardy, unless Jerry, Elaine, George, and Kramer can fight their way through the crowd to the counter!

WINE

CAKE

CINNAMON

CHOCOLATE BABKA $5

VODKA

BUDWAIS

COLD BEER

LIQUOR

OPEN

George scored VIP seats for his friends next to the team owner. But Kramer's antics in the stands have made him a video scoreboard phenomenon, and Elaine and Jerry want to return their nachos to the snack stand. If their seats stay empty, George will hear it from the image-conscious owner!

HUNAN 5TH AVENUE RESTAURANT

We're very busy tonight; there are no tables available just now. Should be five, ten minutes. Your name, please? Feel free to use our pay phone as you wait. Or look around, maybe you'll see someone you know. Just don't take egg rolls off their plates. Cartwright! Party of four!

NBC OFFICES

Jerry and George are late for a big pitch meeting with important network executives, but they're lost in a maze of cubicles. Kramer and Elaine, who accompanied their friends, are desperately trying to find them, creating prime-time pandemonium wherever they go. Television may never be the same again!

THE CAR DEALERSHIP

Jerry's "insider deal" on a new car is on the rocks now that car sales-man Puddy and Elaine have broken up. Jerry's trying to negotiate new terms for their relationship while George searches everywhere for the candy bar that should have rightfully been his.

PUERTO RICAN DAY PARADE ROUTE

The turnout to celebrate Puerto Rico this year is huge . . . and our crabby quartet are stuck somewhere in the middle of it! Maroon Golf is completely unsympathetic and escaping under the bleachers is a dead end. If only they had a laser pointer to show them the way!

THE COURTHOUSE

Jerry and the gang are on trial for cracking jokes during a carjacking rather than trying to prevent it. The jury doesn't look very forgiving, the character witnesses are more than ready to testify against them, Jackie Chiles wants his retainer fee, and someone's stolen the judge's gavel! Order in the court!

Checklists

When you're done searching for Jerry, Elaine, George, and Kramer,
see if you can find these additional items.

JERRY'S APARTMENT
- ❏ Superman Figurine
- ❏ Jerry's Computer
- ❏ Empty Cereal Box
- ❏ "#1 Dad" T-shirt
- ❏ Bicycle
- ❏ Kramer's Shower Hose
- ❏ Fusilli Jerry
- ❏ Cigar Roller/Revolutionary Leader
- ❏ Red Kettle
- ❏ Cat and Cow Oven Mitts

MONK'S CAFÉ
- ❏ Monk's Menu
- ❏ Reggie's Menu
- ❏ Kelly's Handmade Hair Clips
- ❏ Rubber Band in Soup Bowl
- ❏ Babu's Visa Renewal Form
- ❏ Red Ketchup Squirt Bottle
- ❏ Yellow Mustard Squirt Bottle
- ❏ Big Salad
- ❏ Egg-White Omelet
- ❏ Coat Rack

J. PETERMAN CATALOG OFFICES
- ❏ J. Peterman Company Jacket
- ❏ Executive Line Raincoat
- ❏ Mud-Spattered Pants
- ❏ Urban Sombrero
- ❏ Burma Travel Poster
- ❏ "Sack Lunch" Movie Poster
- ❏ Susie's Funeral Wreath
- ❏ King Edward's Wedding Cake
- ❏ JFK's Golf Clubs
- ❏ Mongolian Horsehair Vest

JERRY'S PARENTS' DEL BOCA VISTA PHASE III COMMUNITY
- ❏ Wizard Personal Digital Assistant
- ❏ Kramer's Shoes
- ❏ Morty's Wallet
- ❏ Kramer Campaign Poster
- ❏ Jerry's Culottes
- ❏ Suitcase Filled with Cereal Boxes
- ❏ Astronaut Pen
- ❏ Barbell
- ❏ Cadillac Keys

GEORGE'S PARENTS' HOUSE
- ❏ Mousetrap
- ❏ The Bro/Manssiere
- ❏ George's Seventh Birthday Cake
- ❏ TV Guide Volume 41, number 31
- ❏ Mushy Meatloaf
- ❏ Frank's Cabana Wear
- ❏ Kruger Industrial Smoothing Brochure
- ❏ Festivus Pole
- ❏ Human Fund Donation Card

ELAINE'S APARTMENT
- ❏ Pencil Sharpener
- ❏ Candy Bar, Fork, and Knife
- ❏ J. Peterman Catalog
- ❏ Framed New Yorker Cartoon
- ❏ Possibly Rabid Dog
- ❏ Bowl of Lobster Bisque
- ❏ Cashmere Sweater with Red Dot
- ❏ Box of Jujyfruits
- ❏ Elaine Look-Alike Mannequin
- ❏ Goldfish in a Bag
- ❏ Kramer's Coffee Table Book

GEORGE'S APARTMENT

- ❑ Bubble Boy
- ❑ Jerk Store Bag
- ❑ Box of Wedding Invitations
- ❑ Pendant Publishing Cleaning Woman
- ❑ Bowl of Shrimp
- ❑ Golf Ball
- ❑ Rageaholics Anonymous Chip
- ❑ Chiropractor Bill
- ❑ Tip Jar
- ❑ Wheelchair

ROYAL BAKERY/SCHNITZER'S

- ❑ Black-and-White Cookie
- ❑ George's Gore-Tex Jacket
- ❑ Babka
- ❑ Bottle of Soda
- ❑ Take-a-Number Ticket Dispenser
- ❑ Jar of Cinnamon
- ❑ Walking Boot
- ❑ Saddam Hussein
- ❑ Giant-Size Can of Beef-A-Reeno
- ❑ Marble Rye

BASEBALL STADIUM

- ❑ Stuffed Rooster
- ❑ Calzone
- ❑ Broken, Empty Trophy Case
- ❑ Magnifying Glass
- ❑ Bobblehead Doll
- ❑ SP-2000 Bomb Defusing Robot
- ❑ Chainsaw
- ❑ T-Shirt Cannon
- ❑ Ice Cream Vendor
- ❑ Face-Painted Puddy and Pals

SOUP NAZI SOUP KITCHEN

- ❑ Newman
- ❑ Uncle Leo
- ❑ Soup Nazi Neckerchief
- ❑ Kenny Bania
- ❑ Ladle
- ❑ Box of Plastic Spoons
- ❑ Bowl of Lima Beans
- ❑ Travel Magazine
- ❑ Couch Cushion
- ❑ "Know Your Soup" Sign

HUNAN 5TH AVENUE RESTAURANT

- ❑ Menu
- ❑ Pay Phone
- ❑ Roll of Quarters
- ❑ Plate of Egg Rolls
- ❑ Reservation Book
- ❑ "Please Wait to Be Seated" Sign
- ❑ George's Address Book
- ❑ Host
- ❑ Plate of Sea Bass
- ❑ "Tonight's Specials" Board

NBC OFFICES

- ❑ Radar Detector
- ❑ Motorcycle Helmet
- ❑ "Crazy" Joe Davola
- ❑ "La Cocina" Program
- ❑ Pilot Script
- ❑ Box of Raisins
- ❑ Russell Dalrymple's Daughter
- ❑ Kramer Wanted Poster
- ❑ Plate of Pasta Primavera
- ❑ Greenpeace Brochure

THE CAR DEALERSHIP

- ❑ Tire Display
- ❑ Candy Bar
- ❑ Customer Service Window
- ❑ Watercooler
- ❑ "Salesman of the Month" Plaque
- ❑ Coffee Machine
- ❑ Copier
- ❑ Box of Donuts
- ❑ Clipboard
- ❑ Adding Machine

PUERTO RICAN DAY PARADE ROUTE

- ❑ Laser Pointer
- ❑ *Blimp* Movie Billboard
- ❑ Drum Player
- ❑ Dog Walker
- ❑ "Apartment for Sale" Sign
- ❑ Churro Cart
- ❑ Puerto Rican Flag Vendor
- ❑ Priest
- ❑ Mirrored Sunglasses

THE COURTHOUSE

- ❑ Swiss Cheese
- ❑ *Latham Ledger* Newspaper
- ❑ Gavel
- ❑ Key Ring
- ❑ Court Reporter
- ❑ Juror Badge
- ❑ Video Camera
- ❑ Dartboard
- ❑ Joe Bookman, Library Cop
- ❑ Judge Vandelay's Globe

Key

JERRY'S APARTMENT

JERRY'S APARTMENT

A burst pipe in Jerry's building has made life miserable for many residents, but Jerry's place isn't affected. Good Samaritan Kramer has invited everyone to Jerry's for relief. Even the Cuban cigar rollers have come! Now they're all eating Jerry's cereal, there's a long line for the bathroom, and Kramer's hiding from Jerry's wrath!

MONK'S CAFÉ

MONK'S CAFÉ

The "Big Salad Special" has packed the diner with hungry customers, and some of them are familiar faces. Is that an old boyfriend of Elaine's? How did Kramer already get a seat? And are the Bizarro versions of the gang trying to beat our heroes to their favorite booth?

J. PETERMAN CATALOG OFFICES

JERRY'S PARENTS' DEL BOCA VISTA PHASE III COMMUNITY

GEORGE'S PARENTS' HOUSE

ELAINE'S APARTMENT

GEORGE'S APARTMENT

ROYAL BAKERY/SCHNITZER'S

SOUP NAZI SOUP KITCHEN

HUNAN 5TH AVENUE RESTAURANT

NBC OFFICES

THE CAR DEALERSHIP

THE CAR DEALERSHIP

Jerry's "insider deal" on a new car is on the rocks now that car salesman Puddy and Elaine have broken up. Jerry's trying to negotiate new terms for their relationship while George searches everywhere for the candy bar that should have rightfully been his.

PUERTO RICAN DAY PARADE ROUTE

PUERTO RICAN DAY PARADE ROUTE

The turnout to celebrate Puerto Rico this year is huge . . . and our crabby quartet are stuck somewhere in the middle of it! Maroon Golf is completely unsympathetic and escaping under the bleachers is a dead end. If only they had a laser pointer to show them the way!

THE COURTHOUSE

Jerry and the gang are on trial for cracking jokes during a carjacking rather than trying to prevent it. The jury doesn't look very forgiving, the character witnesses are more than ready to testify against them, Jackie Chiles wants his retainer fee, and someone's stolen the judge's gavel! Order in the court!